Hey! Don't just sit there... Let's have some fun!

With thanks to Ien de Jong

First American Edition 2004
by Kane/Miller Book Publishers, Inc.
La Jolla, California

© 2002 Text and Illustrations: Ferry Piekart & Lars Deltrap
© 2002 Uitgeverij J.H Gottmer / H.J.W. Becht bv, Haarlem, the Netherlands
Originally published under the title: Paf, af!
© 2003 English Translation: Lorraine T. Miller & Ferry Piekart
Original design: Evelien van der Zaken

Library of Congress Control Number: 2003109287
Printed and Bound in China by Regent Publishing Services Ltd.
1 2 3 4 5 6 7 8 9 10

ISBN 1-929132-62-X

Playing With Stuff

Outrageous Games with Ordinary Objects

Ferry Piekart and Lars Deltrap

Translated by Lorraine T. Miller

Kane/Miller BOOK PUBLISHERS

Playing With Stuff

What kind of crazy book is this, anyway?

No, you don't need a super-deluxe, specially-carved waffle whistle, or an extra-special, self-propelling miniature hammer. You don't even need a pair of fork-tongued turf pliers. To play these games, all you need is a bunch of ordinary objects. Stuff. The sort of things everyone has lying around the house. You can play Cheese Squeeze with a slice of cheese and some straws, and then try Snipper Chips with a bag of potato chips and a couple of books. A plain T-shirt is perfect for Bumple Rumple, and Furniture Fuddle can be done in almost any room. In fact, you'll discover that your whole house is filled with wonderful game stuff! Just look at all the fun you can have. It's right here in this book.

But wait! Watch out! Once you've started reading, the trash can will become your worst enemy. Honestly! Along with your parents, of course, who throw out everything – soda cans, old calendars, empty toilet paper rolls – there it all goes, right into the trash, as if it's…*garbage! Outrageous!*

It's not your parents' fault, though. They really don't know any better. It's not as if they realize this is the stuff that games are made of. No one ever told them that empty toilet paper rolls are perfect for *Rabbit Runnel*. Or that an absolutely terrific game of *Calendar Caper* is simple if you save old calendars. And let's not forget *Scatter Clatter* with a pile of empty soda cans! Parents don't have a clue! It's understandable, given that these games have never been written down before, or even mentioned. Until now. Take advantage of it! (And, while you're thinking about it, why not memorize some of these games for a rainy day? Of course, they're great for sunny days too!) You'll always have something to do.

Look around your house to see what kind of stuff you have on hand. Then, check the index at the back of this book to see which games you can play right away. It's a good idea to write out what you need for the games on a piece of paper (just don't tear the index out of the book!). Hang your list by the trash can in your house so all those disgustingly tidy people you live with will know exactly what not to throw away!

Are you ready for some serious fun? One last warning is required. These games have one drawback: in the end, someone will lose.

But, don't give up. Keep *Playing with Stuff!*

It could be YOU!

GAMES

Bumple Rumple

Riding for hours in the car isn't much fun. Standing in an endless line for the roller coaster is even worse. Waiting is horrible! It's awful! The pits! Except when you can pass the time with a rousing round of *Bumple Rumple*. All of a sudden waiting is fun! And luckily you can *Bumple Rumple* just about anywhere.

Actually, you've always had the game *Bumple Rumple* with you. You just didn't know it. All you need is a plain old T-shirt, a sweater or a blouse. In fact, you're probably wearing one of those. Now for the game. Collect some stuff that happens to be lying around near you. Make sure the other player doesn't see what you're gathering up. (He's going to have to guess what those things are!) Pick something and hide it under your shirt. Push the object forward so the shape is clearly visible under your shirt. Can the other player guess what it is? Then it's his turn and you have to guess.

Be Careful!

It's strictly forbidden to rumple with an elephant under your shirt (bicycles are allowed).

Robber Roundup

Bank robbers, jewel thieves and cat burglars on the prowl for great treasures all practice in the same way – with toilet paper! Yes, toilet paper is the perfect training stuff for shifty types. But toilet paper training is fun for us law-abiding types too. *Robber Roundup* doesn't have to be practice for… robbing. It's also just an *outrageous* game.

Most likely you've seen it in the movies – when a burglar breaks into a building there's usually high-tech security. Laser beams criss-cross the entire place and the slightest touch triggers the alarm: beep-beep-peep! Tatuu-tatuuuuh! Risky business. That's why real robbers practice. And you can too (even though you're not a robber). How? With lots of toilet paper of course!

Take long strips of toilet paper and, stretching them, criss-cross them throughout the room. Make sure the room is completely covered just like in this drawing. Also make sure the strips of paper are stretched as tightly as possible. That way they'll break easily (beep-beep-peep) if someone brushes up against them. Secure the ends of the toilet paper around the knobs and the legs of furniture. (Taping toilet paper to the walls or furniture isn't a very good idea. You don't want to leave any evidence behind!)

Make sure your CD player is on one side of the room. The "robber" whose turn it is then goes to the other side. Someone else now turns on the music. The person whose turn it is (the cat burglar for instance) has as much time as the song lasts to get to the CD side of the room without tearing a single strip of paper! The toilet paper can't rip and it can't come loose. If this happens then the person is out. But if the "robber" makes it across the room then cutting off the alarm (stopping the music!), is obviously the first task at hand. The CD display indicates how long it has taken to bypass the security system.

Professional robbers regularly use this as a test to screen new recruits. That's why it's called *Robber Roundup*. They pretend the CD player is the alarm that must be shutdown. Which of the robbers in your gang is fastest on their feet?

Handy Hint!
No CD player at hand? No problem! You can play with a cassette player as well. Just play the tape, push "pause" when you reach the cassette player, and remember on which moment in the song you did so! Are the others faster or not?

Stress Guess

This game should only be played by people who can deal well with stress. After all, it's called *Stress Guess*. What? You've never heard of it? Of course you haven't! It's new! It's only just been invented! It's nerve wracking! It's stressful! Do you dare to give it a go?

Set the kitchen timer for one minute. Double check that it will actually buzz or ring once this minute has passed. Now quickly, hide the timer! You're not allowed to look at it anymore. From now on everyone has to keep track of the time in their head. When you think a minute has passed shout "now!" If the kitchen timer goes off immediately after that then you're a genius at telling time. But don't despair. Nobody's timing is perfect.

Here comes the stress part. The person who shouts "now!" closest to the timer going off is the winner. Once it has gone off you're not allowed to shout anymore. No shouting while the timer is ringing either. You must guesstimate the right moment to shout "now!" - just before the minute is up.

One Extra Rule:
You're only allowed to shout "now!" twice in each round. Otherwise it's just too easy and everyone shouts "now, now, now!" the entire time. So twice is the maximum. Nerve-racking? Stressful? We told you so!

Pingshot

Pingshot is the only target practice game in the world where the aim is not to aim at all. "You mean we don't have to hit anything? What about a target? A dartboard? The bull's-eye?" No. None of those. The idea is not to hit anything, but to lose everything. Then you'll be a pro at _Pingshot_!

What will you need?

* film canisters
  (the plastic kind with lids)
* a messy room
* an opponent
* a watch

When you buy a roll of 35mm film it usually comes in a hard plastic canister with a lid. These generally go right into the garbage. What a shame! You should save stuff like this because the flip-top lids are really great for pinging. Have any canisters lying around? Grab one. Does it still have a lid? Good. Now push hard with your thumb against the middle of the canister. Ping! The lid shoots off (probably in the direction you least expected). If you were standing in a basement or attic filled with junk there's a good chance you'd never locate that lid again. Precisely the idea!

Go with your opponent and find a really messy room. Decide who will go first. That player is the shooter. The other person is the seeker. Once the shooter has pinged the lid you both go look for it. If neither of you can find the lid after one minute then the shooter wins. (Keep track of the time on your watch.) If the shooter does find the lid then he gets to ping it off again. If the seeker finds the lid you reverse roles: the seeker becomes the shooter and the shooter becomes the seeker.

Tip:
Having problems pinging your lid? Try a sturdier plastic canister or one from a different brand of film.

Furniture Fuddle

People all over the world are already playing this game. In Germany it's called **Führnitur Fudel**, in Denmark it's **Fødel Furnitør**, and in France it's called **Fuddle du Furniteur**. Here it's *Furniture Fuddle* but it's an *outrageous* game in any language.

You'll need this:

* a room full of furniture
* someone else who wants to play
* useful: a referee (whistle not required)

You should perfect your game of *Furniture Fuddle* as quickly as possible.

It's getting to be mega-popular! Wherever you go, whatever you do, you could find yourself in a situation where you have to *Furniture Fuddle*. You don't want people to think you're out of it. Practice!

Examine the room you're in right now and make an exact mental picture in your mind of where all the furniture is standing. When we say exact we mean EXACT! Now, one of the players leaves the room. That person is the Guesser. The other person is the Mover.

The Mover chooses a chair, table, lamp, or other piece of furniture and moves it a few inches. Then the Guesser comes back into the room. She has to play detective, taking a good look around the room and trying to figure out which piece of furniture has been moved. Only one guess is allowed. Is it wrong? Then the Guesser leaves the room again. The Mover moves the displaced piece of furniture a few inches farther (you're not allowed to put it back where it was; you have to keep moving it in the same direction). Then the Guesser comes back into the room and has to guess for the second time. Wrong again? She has to leave the room again. The Mover moves the piece of furniture another few inches. And this is how it goes until the Guesser finally gets it right. Then you reverse roles. Who needs the least amount of turns to guess correctly? Keep track!

Want to make it harder?

Try playing Furniture Fuddle *in a furniture store. First politely ask the store's customers not to buy any sofas or anything for a little while. Ask if they wouldn't mind not touching the furniture for the time being either! Do tell them it's for playing a round of* Furniture Fuddle. *Then they'll be much more cooperative.*

Rabbit Runnel

You'll need this:

* 2 rubber bands
* 1 short piece of string
* 2 empty toilet paper tubes
* wooden blocks
* other people who like playing tag

Face it, ordinary tag is a pretty boring game. Who wants to run around and around in circles? You think it's boring too? Then you're probably ready for a good game of _Rabbit Runnel_. It's a completely new take on tag.

Rabbits hardly ever play tag. No, not because they're harebrained. It's because their eyes aren't in the right place for it. A rabbit's eyes are on the sides of its head. Rabbits can see what's happening to the right and to the left but not what's right in front of their noses. This makes running after someone extremely difficult. That's the real reason rabbits don't like playing tag.

It's funny to see the world from a rabbit's eye-view. _Rabbit Runnel_ goggles make it possible. The drawing on this page shows you exactly how to make a pair. You'll need to poke 2 holes in each of the tubes, then you use the string to tie the tubes together and the rubber bands to hold the tubes over your ears (make a knot in one end). When you're finished just put them on and start playing tag! You'll soon discover it isn't as easy as it looks!

Of course, everyone who wants to play has to wear a pair of _Rabbit Runnel_ goggles.

Be careful!

Wear your Rabbit Runnel goggles only in safe places where there isn't any traffic and you won't keep running into things. The park is a good place.

Tower Tunnel

Put on your Rabbit Runnel goggles and play Tower Tunnel. Try building a tower of wooden blocks while wearing your Rabbit Runnel goggles. It isn't easy! Compete against each other Who can build a tower of ten wooden blocks the fastest? If you knock them over just start again!

Clammy Claw

Is it possible to lift stuff with your fingertips? No, of course not! Stuff doesn't stick to people's fingers just like that. Well, not unless you've just finished a really gooey peanut butter & jelly sandwich. That might work. Other than that, fingertips only work for picking stuff up if you're *Clammy Clawing*.

Clammy Claw is a competition, so it's played against someone else. Before you begin, place the scale in the middle of the table. Line up all kinds of small things along the table's edge (pens, pencils, erasers, coins, paper clips… it doesn't really matter what, as long as there's lots of stuff). The game begins with you and your opponent each attaching photo tabs to the fingers of one of your hands. Each fingertip gets one of these adhesives. Then, taking turns, you have to pick up one of the small objects on the table and place it on the scale. You're not allowed to use your hands to pick up or grab anything though – stuff has to stick to the tips of your fingers. You can apply a little bit of pressure so the stuff sticks better but you can't do anything else.

When you place the object on the scale write down its weight, then put it to one side out of the game (you can use your hands to do this). Keep taking turns until you've used up all the stuff on the table, then add up how much weight each of you has placed on the scale. The person with the most weight wins.

A few more rules:

If you have something stuck to your fingers and it falls off, you lose your turn. That object is removed from the game and then it's the other player's turn. By the way, stuff shouldn't fall onto the scale; you have to place it there carefully. If you try to put something on the scale and it's still sticking, then it's okay to use your other hand to remove it from your fingertips.

Rattle Racket

Want to play a great game and at the same time drive your family completely insane? No problem! When you play *Rattle Racket* they'll go crazy!

What will you need?

* 1 plastic 2 liter soda bottle (empty!!!)
* 1 marble
* a helpful grownup

A plastic soda bottle needs to be cut in half with a very sharp knife. You're a smart kid, so let your father or mother or some other helpful grown-up do this for you. Then if there's a slip-up they'll end up cutting themselves (ouch!), and you won't. Ask them to slice the bottle in half under the neck. Then set the 2 halves upside down inside of each other (just like in the drawing).

The game can begin! Drop the marble into the bottle through the open half. Now for the hard part – try removing the marble! You can only do this by shaking the bottle. It's pretty difficult. In the beginning, you'll rattle and rattle until you're exhausted from rattling. What a racket! (That's also why it's called *Rattle Racket*) Our advice? Keep playing with this stuff! The more you practice the faster you'll be able to remove the marble.

Rattle Battle:
It's even more fun to make 2 Rattle Racket bottles and compete against another player. Then it's called Rattle Battle. The player who removes their marble first is the winner. You make twice the racket though, so don't be surprised if your neighbors end up with cotton balls sticking out of their ears.

cut the bottle
in half here

take the cap off

then put it back
together like this

Snipper Chips

What will you need?

* a bag of potato chips
* pen and paper
* a small book
* a not-so-small book
* an utterly not-so-small book
* another person to play with

Snipper Chips has got to be the most smashing chip game of all time. What do you have to do? It's simple – smash some chips to bits. (No, it doesn't matter if they're plain potato chips or barbecue potato chips.)

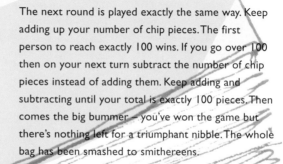

When you drop a book on top of a potato chip, it shatters (the chip that is, not the book). That's *Snipper Chips* exactly! Take a potato chip out of the bag and place it on the table. Then pick a book (a small book, a not-so-small book, or an utterly not-so-small book) to smash the chip. Drop the book on top of the chip and then count the number of chip pieces and write them down Then it's the other player's turn to smash a chip with a book.

pieces smaller than this don't count

The next round is played exactly the same way. Keep adding up your number of chip pieces. The first person to reach exactly 100 wins. If you go over 100 then on your next turn subtract the number of chip pieces instead of adding them. Keep adding and subtracting until your total is exactly 100 pieces. Then comes the big bummer – you've won the game but there's nothing left for a triumphant nibble. The whole bag has been smashed to smithereens.

Klutz Futz

Klutz Futz **is played between 2 clods and a futzing klutz. It's actually played in the same old cloddy way as traditional Futz only you need a lot less space.**

You'll need this:

* a 12" x 3" strip of sturdy cardboard
* a table
* scissors
* a small ball
* your index finger
* someone else's index finger
* the index finger of another person
(leave the fingers attached to the players!)

Start with a sturdy piece of cardboard approximately 12 inches long and 3 inches wide. Using a pair of scissors make 3 holes in this cardboard strip, one exactly in the middle and one near each of the ends. The holes have to be large enough so that an index finger can fit through them. All the players sit or stand next to each other behind a table. Place the strip of cardboard on the table. The clod sitting to the right puts his index finger through the left hole; the clod to the left puts her index finger through the right hole. This leaves the person sitting in the middle to put his index finger through the middle hole. Ha Ha! Now it's official! The futzing klutz lives!

Now comes the actual futzing around with the ball. The left clod and the right clod pass the ball back and forth between themselves with their index fingers. The futzing klutz in the middle tries to stop the ball with his index finger. Success? Then the clod that touched the ball last has to switch places with the futzing klutz.

More rules:
The clods and the futzing klutz are only allowed to touch the ball with their index fingers. If the clods aren't very skillful at passing the ball back and forth and the ball zooms by them or shoots off the table 3 times in a row, then the futzing klutz is allowed to choose a new futzing klutz (although he doesn't have to)!

15

Water Waddle

You'll need this:

* a stack of plastic cups
* buckets (2 per player)
* loose-fitting socks
* water
* a stopwatch or timer
* people you can beat

Have you ever been in one of those races where you have to balance an egg on a spoon while holding the spoon between your teeth? What a boring game! You know why? Nobody can laugh! The spoon would fall out of their mouths! Please... how can a game be fun if you can't even laugh? Play *Water Waddle* instead – you can laugh your head off!

Now pay close attention because we're only going to explain this once. All the players should be wearing a pair of loose-fitting socks. Put a plastic cup - with the opening facing up - inside each of your socks. Next you have to choose a spot for the starting line. Everyone sets their own bucket on that line. Approximately 15 feet away is the finish line. Everyone should place a bucket there as well. The starting line buckets need to be filled with water - exactly the same amount in each. Now the game can begin! You all go and stand by your start buckets and take a third plastic cup in your hand. It's time to start the timer or stopwatch. Fill the plastic cups in your socks with water using the third cup you are holding. Carefully waddle off to your finish line bucket and pour the water into it. Then it's back to the starting line and the whole thing starts again.

Note:

You're not allowed to use your hands when you empty the water cups in your socks! You have to come up with a way to pour the water using your feet! You only have 2 minutes to waddle back and forth! (Someone should keep track of the time.) The player who has the most water in their finish line bucket after 2 minutes is the Water Waddle *winner!*

Bash Ball

What will you need?

* 2 tennis balls
* 1 piece of rope, 6 feet long
* a big roll of tape (duct tape is best)
* 2 Bash Ball teams

Please don't get angry at us for saying this, but soccer is such a predictable game. The ball usually only goes in the direction it's kicked. With *Bash Ball* though, it's all different. Kick the ball to your left, and there's a good chance it'll go to the right – or straight ahead! It's not predictable at all! It's completely *outrageous!*

What makes *Bash Ball* so hilarious is that the game is played with 2 balls, attached to each other by a piece of rope. If you give one of the balls a powerful kick there's a good chance it'll go in the opposite direction you were expecting, because someone else just kicked the other ball at the same time. Tricky stuff, huh?

Okay listen, first you have to attach the tennis balls to each other. Tie one end of the rope around the first ball. Wrap a whole lot of tape around it, so it can't possibly come loose. Attach the other end of the rope to the second ball in exactly the same way. Now the game can begin.

Bash Ball is played just like soccer: 2 teams, 2 goals…but 2 balls! Oh yes, be careful, don't trip over the rope and bash yourself in the head!

Topsy Tumble

"The world is flat. If you're not careful you'll fall right off the edge." Not so very long ago, people thought this was the truth. Hard to believe? Duh! What a bunch of Simple Simon's they were! Still, it did give us a good idea for a game. In *Topsy Tumble*, you have the world at your fingertips... just make sure nobody tumbles off!

You'll need this:

* a large, flat, pan lid
* lots of toy people
  (LEGO® or Playmobil® figures work well – it doesn't matter as long as they can stand up)
* some sturdy string
* someone else who wants to play

The lid of a large saucepan or frying pan serves as the flattened world. Hang it from something using a piece of sturdy string. (Don't attach it to a costly lamp though; it's better to pick the limb of a tree or a ladder.) You don't have to do much of anything else except find someone to play with you (no kidnapping!). Each of you get half of the tiny people and you take turns carefully setting them up one at a time on the wobbly pan lid. The first player to make a figure topple off the edge loses. In this world, you not only have to hang in there, you have to hang on!

coins
broom
wall
cans
plate
pans
paper
book
soup bowl
confetti
umbrella
letter scale
make-up
pogo stick
straws
chesspawns
daffodils
cheese
cassette tapes
potato chips
serving tray
stickers
envelopes
pencil case
dice
rubber bands
bucket
Boston cream pie
scissors
overnight bag
magic markers
chessboard
shoes
fruit bowl
watch
pack of sprink
cardboard
clock
gol
kn
to
ru
la
ba   b

You'll need this:

* junk mail
  (store flyers with pictures of stuff)
* a marker
* a small piece of paper
* someone else into playing Ad Sav

Some games take just fifteen minutes to play. Others can last an hour or more. Some even take a whole day. That's nothing compared to this junk mail marathon. *Ad Sav* is about the bigger picture. It can take a week (or even a month) to play. Don't worry. Even if it does last that long, you'll just barely have to exert yourself. Thank goodness, right?

Ad Sav appears in your mailbox absolutely free of charge. It's true. All you need to play is junk mail. You know the kind we mean, the supermarket and drugstore flyers with pictures of all kinds of store-sale stuff. Each player picks a flyer and circles 5 things. Now you have to memorize what you've circled because Ad Sav is a memory game. Exchange flyers and hide your opponent's in a safe place so she won't be able to find it. A week or so later you should meet up again. Now you have to think back and name the 5 things you circled. Which of you has the best memory? The person who can remember the most items wins. Naturally, cheating is strictly forbidden. No secretly jotting down what you've circled in your flyer. If you're caught, the penalty is memorizing 347 things and then having to recite them aloud 5 hours later. Poking around in your opponent's house to look for signs of cheating is permitted. You're also allowed to write down the date on a piece of paper, so you don't forget when you're supposed to continue playing. (That would be a shame!) Hang the reminder in a noticeable spot.

Tip for skilled *Ad Sav* fanatics:
If you want to make the game even harder, you can circle more than 5 items. 10, for example. (That's a lot of stuff!) Or you can wait a longer period of time, not a week but a month (or more). Or do both: memorize 10 things and then wait a month.

Zany Zapping

What will you need?

* the remote control
* 10 fingers (9 won't work)
* someone to make things difficult for you

Your little finger usually just hangs around, not doing much of anything. As a finger it's a waste of time – unless you're a pinky ring. Or unless you want to play *Zany Zapping* – then suddenly it's the most important finger on your hand. The problem is it's also the most uncooperative…

Ordinarily you only push the buttons on your remote control one at a time. Not in *Zany Zapping*. In this game you eventually have to push all 10 buttons at the same time. That is, if you can manage! Place the remote in front of you. (You start because you're the one reading this.) The other person is there to make the game as difficult as possible for you. This annoying person chooses a button on the remote control like the fast-forward-button, (if there is one, of course), or the volume-louder-button. You have to press that button with one of your fingers. It's your choice which finger you use first. Once you've done this your opponent selects another button. You have to push that button with a different finger. You still have 9 fingers left so you have more than enough choices! That's how this game goes. It gets harder and harder – because you're not allowed to remove your fingers from the buttons you've already touched. If that happens, you're out!

So why is it called *Pinky Piddle* in other parts of the country? Because there's one more outrageous rule: you're required to save a pinky for last. The 10th button must be pressed with one of your little fingers. Left or right pinky, it doesn't matter which. Have fun. Who will get the most fingers on the buttons? Will anyone take control with 10?

Calendar Caper

Did your parents already get rid of last year's calendar? What a crime! An old calendar is exactly what you need to play a terrific game of *Calendar Caper*. Never, ever, throw away old calendars – you'll regret it the rest of the year!

Can you find another old calendar? One your parents missed? You need the kind that has the entire month on one page. Choose your favorite month. This is the board. Put your game pieces on the first day of the month. Now the game can begin. Take turns throwing one of the dice and moving your piece. (If you throw a 5, then you move your game piece forward 5 days.) The date you land on is yours from that moment on! Write your name in its box with a marker. You continue playing like this, taking turns. If you land on a date that doesn't belong to anyone, you write your name there. But if you land on a date that is somebody else's property, well… tough luck, it's worthless! When you get to the last day of the month, you return to the beginning of that same month. You do this until all the days of the month have been claimed. Then each of you adds up your dates. For example, March 3, March 7 March 9, March 10, March 24, March 30, become 3 + 7 + 9 + 10 + 24 + 30 = 83. Make sure to count all of the dates that belong to you. The person with the highest number wins.

Tip: *Did you already make the mistake of throwing out your old calendar? No problem! You can play Calendar Caper with your current calendar, too. Simply choose a month that has already passed. Or play the game using a pencil. You get to erase everyone's name once you've won the game… sorry… not much of a prize!*

Pesty Chess

"Checkmate!" That's what chess players shout when they've won. For the most part though, chess is another one of those dull, boring games. We need more action! Push aside those silly chessmen and play *Pesty Chess* instead!

You'll need this:

* a chessboard
* 8 toy people (Playmobil® or LEGO® work well)
* 4 rubber bands
* 4 push pins
* a ping-pong ball
* an opponent

Chess is a serious minded game. Not *Pesty Chess*. It's a shooting-gallery game, and the aim is to pester your opponent's "pawns". First you have to set up the *Pesty Chess* board, like the one in the drawing below. Stand your men on the spots marked with Xs like in the drawing on the left. Now you're ready to play.

Use the rubber band at your end to launch the ping-pong ball, taking aim at your opponent's men. Watch out! Before you know it you'll be knocking down your own men as well. That's not the idea, because the first player who doesn't have any men left standing loses. Then the winner doesn't shout "Checkmate!" she shouts "Pestmate!" That's the rule!

Too easy? Need more of a challenge? Try using fewer men. Or set up the board differently.

set up your toy figures like this:

22

Cheese Squeeze

Why does some cheese have holes? Because someone on the Swiss-cheese-making farm started playing a game of *Cheese Squeeze* and didn't have time to finish. Now it's up to you!

You'll need this:

* a slice of cheese
* a small plate   * 2 straws
* someone else who wants to play...again...sigh

Are you ready to squeeze some cheese?

Place a slice of cheese on a small plate and pick a straw (not the cocktail kind, otherwise you'll be playing this game forever!). Alternating turns, you now make a hole in the cheese using the tip of your straw. It's the best technique there is for making lovely round holes in the cheese; holes which are also delicious to eat, so feel free! The object of the game is simple: the person who cannot squeeze another single, solitary hole out of the cheese because there's no room left, loses! Half a hole doesn't count. Holes that overlap don't qualify either! Only beautiful round holes count. You must carefully calculate where to put all of your holes. Make sure you're not the first one who can't squeeze the cheese!

Balliards

Billiards is nothing but a group of old fuddie duddies standing around, hitting giant marbles with a stick. Why is it called Billiards? What do bills have to do with it? Absolutely nothing! It does have something to do with balls though. It should be called *Balliards* instead of Billiards! Don't you agree? And while we're at it, let's make it easier to play!

You'll need this:

* a table   * a few books   * a pencil
* *Scotch*® brand tape (or similar)
* some paper   * a marker
* a tennis ball   * a large wooden spoon
* a worthy opponent

Have your table sit at an angle by putting a few books under 2 of the legs. Make sure that one side of the table is about 6 inches higher than the other. Tape some sheets of paper together and, using a marker, divide the sheet into 4 sections exactly like in the drawing. Attach the paper to the table using tape. Write "100 points" in the top section, "50 points" in the section under that, then "25 points," and in the last box, write "10 points." Tape a pencil to the very bottom end of the table (just like in the drawing, too). Your *Balliard* table is now complete and the game can begin!

You'll have the most fun if you play against someone else. Take turns placing the ball in front of the pencil and use the wooden spoon as a cue stick. Give the ball a push with the spoon. The higher it goes the more points you get. Careful! If the ball flies off the table you don't get any points at all. That's just how it goes in the game of *Balliards*. Sure, this doesn't happen in Billiards because there's an edge around the outside of the table. But, like we already said, that's a game for old fuddie duddies!

Wager Wok

Are you a gambler at heart? They won't let you play in Las Vegas, so get a wok, a fruit bowl, or something similar from the kitchen and make your very own Vegas with _Wager Wok_!

What will you need?

* a wok, a fruit bowl, or something similar
* a marble * 8 wooden toothpicks
* 8 squares of masking tape and/or sticky labels
* pen and paper
* other people brave enough to bet

Attach the 8 toothpicks to the wok, just like in the drawing (you can use tape or extra stickers to do this). Now you have 8 slots. Give each slot its own number - use the stickers to do this. Your _Wager Wok_ is ready. The gambling can begin! There are 2 ways to wager, so you'll have to choose which way you prefer.

Betting even or uneven:
You bet on whether the ending number will be even or uneven; if you choose even you will win if the marble lands in the 2, the 4, the 6, or the 8 slot. When you bet uneven you will win with a 1, a 3, a 5, or a 7. If you've wagered right you get 2 points.

Betting a number:
Here you bet on a specific number. Choose a number from 1 to 8. Your chances of getting it right are much smaller than when you bet even or uneven. It's much harder, but if you do get it right you receive a lot more points — 10, to be exact!

All the gamblers must decide how they're going to bet at the beginning of each throw. Jot down everyone's bet on a piece of paper. Hold the marble on the edge of the pan and give it a good spin so it begins to roll around and around the top of the wok. Once it stops rolling it will end up in one of the slots.

Did you bet an even number and the ball actually landed in an even number slot? Then you've earned 2 points. Did you bet number 3 and the ball has indeed landed in slot number 3? Than you get 10 points! Are you fresh out of luck? Then you get 0 points. Write down everyone's points on a piece of paper and keep a running total. The first person to reach 50 points is the winner.

Story Boardy

You'll need this:

* 1 roll of toilet paper (or maybe a few)
* a marker
* dice (one set per player)
* other people who want to play

We have it on good authority that most kids get really bored playing board games (why else would they be called that?). We also know that you and your friends are the type of kids who always obey the rules. Amazingly boring too! You probably always use the game pieces that come included in the game box, don't you? Get rid of those stupid things! It's time to go wild! It's time to break the rules! Because the playing pieces in this *outrageous* game are life-size and, oh boy, you're all it! Go stand on the game board. "But we're much too big!" As if we can't see that! Stop whining! You don't play *Story Boardy* on just any game board, but on a toilet paper game board!

The first thing you do is lay down a *Story Boardy* "board" running through your entire house. Begin in the kitchen, for example, and end in the bathroom. Lay the toilet paper on the floor, winding it through all the rooms. Use the stairs too – anything is possible! Next you have to divide the game route into big boxes. Using a marker, draw a line after every 6 squares of toilet paper. These are the game boxes. Write instructions in some of these boxes, for example, "roll again" or "go back 5 spaces." Try ridiculous things like "hop on one foot for the rest of the game" or "roll the dice with your toes." Go ahead and make up your own wacky things for the players to do!

Before you begin playing, give everyone their own set of dice. Then take turns rolling your own dice. Walk the number of boxes you've rolled. When you land on a space with instructions you must do as you're told. The player who finishes first is the winner. The player who gets to the end second is second. The player who…well, you get it now, don't you?

return to the start

skip your next turn

roll again

you must roll a 6
to continue

get the other players
something to drink (they
must be thirsty by now!)

go back 5 spaces

only move once all the other
players have passed you

take 2 extra steps

roll the dice with your toes

hop on one foot for the rest of the game

Gaspy Graspy

This is truly a special game. It comes from a secret ritual performed by the infamous Suction Society. Unfortunately, (well, not unfortunately for us), an absent-minded Suction-er, a true enthusiast of the game, accidentally gave it away. Now we can all take part in this *outrageous* ritual. It'll leave you breathless!

You'll need this:

* bendable straws
* scissors
* scraps of paper
* 2 small plates
* a stopwatch, a clock, or a timer
* 1 or more people willing to play.

Gaspy Graspy is simple to play. Place the scraps of paper on a small plate, and put it in the kitchen (or some other room, it doesn't really matter). Put the other plate in another room adjacent to the first one. Now we have to make the *Gaspy Graspy* mouthpiece. Take 4 or 5 bendable straws, and slip them into each other (this works best if you make a small cut with the scissors in each end of the straw). Make sure the straws overlap about an inch or so at each point they slip together, then the mouthpiece will be sturdier. Once they're all together, you should also bend each straw at the joint so the whole thing is curvy. Now you're ready – as soon as someone else agrees to be the Suction Stopwatch-er.

Let the ritual begin! Hold the tube at one end with your hands. Now breathe in really hard, so that one small scrap of paper from the plate is hanging at the end of the straw. Pretty hard with such a bent tube, huh? But the hardest part is still to come: this scrap of paper has to go to the other plate. What's even worse is that all the scraps have to go to the other plate. And you're only allowed to pick them up with your straw. The player who finishes fastest is the winner.

Whirly Swirly

It's true. **Bowling is fun. Playing dominos is fun, too. But** *Whirly Swirly?* **That's some kind of** *outrageous* **game. Especially if you get really good at doing the whirly-curly-domino-swirly.**

You'll need this:

* a floor lamp
* 1 piece of sturdy string (half the length of the lamp)
* 20 cassette tape boxes (it doesn't matter if they're full or empty)
* a roll of Scotch® brand tape (or similar)
* a wily whirly opponent
* 1 or more people willing to play.

First you have to make the whirler, because without it there isn't any game. Tie one end of the string about halfway up the lamp, and then tie the roll of tape to the other end of the string. Your whirler is ready! Stand the cassette boxes on their sides, surrounding the base of the lamp in 2 or 3 circles (like in the drawing). The game can begin!

1. See the light (mandatory!)

2. Give the string a good whirl.

3. If you've whirled well, the string will wind completely around the lamp without knocking over any of the cassette tapes.

4. Now the string will swing back in the other direction and knock over some boxes… as many as possible!

5. The roll of tape on the string will go back and forth a few times. How many cassette boxes are still standing once the roll of tape has stopped whirling and swirling?

6. The idea is to knock over as many of the boxes as you can – more than the other person! Have you done it? If so, then you're simply fabulous at doing the whirly-curly-domino-swirly. And not many people can say that!

Madcapper

Who ever said you have to spray *plants* with a spray bottle? That's no fun at all! Those leaf-covered organic creatures never give in! No matter how hard you spray them, they just won't *fall* over. It's much better to spray at things which don't have irritatingly solid roots. Get ready for some *Madcapping*!

You'll need this:

* lots of bottle caps (all the same color)
* more bottle caps (a different color)
* a spray bottle
* a fence or ledge
* another sharpshooter

Find a fence, ledge, or low wall outside where you can line up all the caps in a single row. Alternate the colors (for example, red-green-red-green-red-green) and leave a little bit of space — an inch or so — between the bottle caps. It's time to take aim! Go stand a little distance away and try to shoot the green caps off the wall using the spray bottle. The red ones should stay put! When you're squirting against another sharpshooter, it's her turn if you accidentally shoot a red bottle cap off the wall. Your opponent continues where you left off. The player to shoot the last green cap off the wall is considered sharpshooter # 1 — and the winner! This *Madcapper* is required to soak the loser until they get really mad. Really! That's what the official rules say! (We're not kidding!)

Sticker Stew

Are you bored? Hanging around? What about a game of *Sticker Stew*? As you're sitting there stewing stickers, you'll think to yourself "Gee whiz, lucky for me that I didn't have a darn thing to do, because *Sticker Stew* is like, really hot stuff."

You'll need this:

* sticky labels
* a small piece of cardboard
* lots of small stuff
* someone else who wants to play, too

First, you have to cook up the *Sticker Stew*. Attach a whole bunch of the labels to the cardboard and each other, overlapping them in all different directions, until you've completely covered the cardboard. You should have a very strange, crazy kind of flat shape, with stickers sticking out here and there. Now, collect a whole bunch of little things, (erasers, paper clips, coins, buttons, that kind of stuff!), then find someone else to play with you. Divide the pile of stuff in half. Taking turns, you each place one of the objects on the strange form you've made. (The strange, *Sticker Stew* stays flat on the table and no one can move it.) In the beginning it's easy. But after a while the form gets full and nothing fits anymore. You're not allowed to put anything even "a tiny bit" on top of anything else, so you must carefully place your stuff in between and around the stuff already there.

WARNING!

Nothing is allowed to slide off the Sticker Stew. Everything has to stay on the stickers. The stuff isn't allowed to overlap the outside edge of the stickers, even the slightest bit. The first person to have something fall off the sticker stew is out. The other person wins the game.

31

Parasol Putt-Putt

Shhh. Don't tell anyone, but *Parasol Putt-Putt* is just ordinary miniature golf, except you don't have to pay to play or get all nervous because there are pushy putters on your heels. *Parasol Putt-Putt* is played in your own backyard.

It's really simple. With the handles of the brooms, rakes, and mops you've collected make a giant rectangle on the ground. You can do this on the grass but on the patio or driveway is probably better. There! Just like that, you've got your own *Parasol Putt-Putt* course. At one end of the course place a dinner plate upside down to use as the hole. It's important that the plate has a rim on the bottom; that way the ball will get caught and not roll off.

At the other end of the course make a small hole in the ground or mark the cement using a piece of chalk. This is the starting point. Place the ball there and you're ready to putt. Use the umbrella as a golf club – you hit the ball with the curved end of the handle.

How many strokes does it take before you manage to land the ball on the plate? The player with the fewest strokes wins. Keep in mind if you hit the ball outside the course, then you get a penalty point (that means you have to add a point to your score).

Practice a lot first, then invite other people to play a round of *Parasol Putt-Putt*. If they ask, "What makes this game so different from miniature golf?" You may reply "Putt-head, you hit the ball with an umbrella!"

For Golf Pros:
Face it, the ordinary 4-sided Parasol Putt-Putt *course is much too easy – it's for beginners. Once you've practiced some you'll be ready for the advanced version,* Parasol Putt-Putt Plus, *with lots of extra obstacles! Surely you can think up some yourselves. We've given you a few good examples in this drawing…*

Note: Although this game is called Parasol Putt-Putt, *for some strange reason you're not allowed to play it with an actual parasol. It's probably because of some government act, written by a long-forgotten politician who was never any good at the game. Therefore, you have to use an umbrella. If someone shows up with a parasol at your* Parasol Putt-Putt *course, tell him it's against the law!*

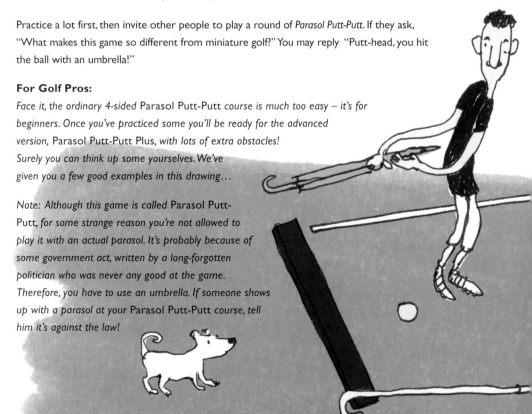

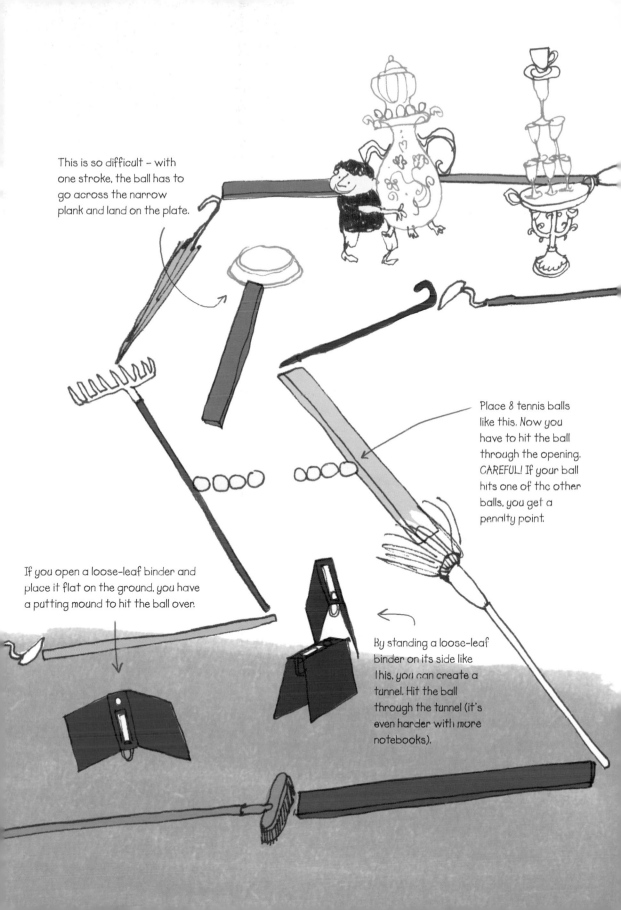

This is so difficult – with one stroke, the ball has to go across the narrow plank and land on the plate.

Place 8 tennis balls like this. Now you have to hit the ball through the opening. CAREFUL! If your ball hits one of the other balls, you get a penalty point.

If you open a loose-leaf binder and place it flat on the ground, you have a putting mound to hit the ball over.

By standing a loose-leaf binder on its side like this, you can create a tunnel. Hit the ball through the tunnel (it's even harder with more notebooks).

Dice Derby

Six inches per hour – not even a snail moves that slowly! But in *Dice Derby*, six inches is a long distance. If you manage that in one turn, wow, you're really covering some territory!

Dice Derby is also different because you race with a ruler. *Dice Derby* is a tiny bit like other board games though. It's played on a board with game pieces and a set of rules. In *Dice Derby* though, a map is the game board, and you pick the game pieces yourself. We've kindly taken care of the detailed rules for you:

1. All the players begin by placing their game pieces on the same spot on the map. Choose a starting destination far away from where you all live. The object of the game is for everybody to set off from the same spot and race to an agreed upon place in your hometown.

2. The players take turns throwing one of the dice. If you throw a 1, then you move 1 inch on the map. Throw a 2 and you can travel 2 inches, and with a 3 you get to journey 3 inches. And that's how all the travelers make their way home, using a ruler to measure the distances. Note: You have to follow the roads on the map!

3. Make a pencil mark on the map where you've landed, and put your game piece there. Erase the mark once you set off for the next destination.

4. Are there railway lines on your map? Use these, they're faster! If you arrive at a spot where a railway line crosses, then with your next turn you can travel along the railway lines. If you travel via the rails, you're allowed to double the amount of inches you throw! So if you throw a 2, you're allowed to move 2 inches twice, or 4 inches in total. (Note: you're only allowed to jump on a train when the road you're traveling on intersects with the railway lines on the map. And like we said, wait until your next turn to travel farther.)

5. Flying is super-sonic! When you arrive at an airport you can use your next turn to fly to another airport closer to home. (You have to throw an even number first though, and you only get one throw per turn.)

6. The first person to arrive home is the winner. And the rest of the players are... not!

Handy hint:

Turn a piece of string into a ruler by making colored marks on the rope to indicate inches. Most roads don't follow a straight line, so it's much easier to measure with a string than with a ruler, and you can easily follow the curves you encounter along the way!

Frozen Towers

You'll need this:

* 20 ice cubes
* someone else who doesn't lose their cool
* a room with air conditioning (optional)

Some games are harder to play when it's warm outside than when it's cold, and *Frozen Towers* is one of them. In the winter it's easy, especially if you play in extremely chilly weather. Then, even an old, wobbly polar bear with the hiccups can play this game. But when you play *Frozen Towers* on a blistering hot day, well, then, it's really *outrageous*!

The object of *Frozen Towers* is to build a tower of ice cubes. Find a good surface and place 4 ice cubes together as the base. Each player then gets 8 ice cubes. Players take turns adding a cube to the tower. The ice cubes are not allowed to slip off.

This isn't difficult if the ice cubes have just come out of the freezer and are still rock hard. You can stack them on top of each other and often they even stick together. Pretty easy! You'll win the first round without any problems. But the second round will be more difficult. The ice cubes will slowly melt. They become slippery, wet and slimy and slide right off each other. The longer the game lasts the more difficult it becomes.

Frozen Towers is meant to be played together. If you succeed in building a tower out of all the ice cubes, then you win the game as a team. But if one of the player's ice cubes slides off, then he or she is the lonely loser (which doesn't make the other player the winner). Weird rule? Sorry, that's just how it goes in the off-the-wall game of *Frozen Towers*.

Scatter Clatter

You'll need this:

* empty soda cans (4 per person)
* pebbles or small stones
* masking tape or duct tape
* people who like playing hide-and-seek

There aren't very many people who *Scatter Clatter*. What a pity. It's such a cheerful game. Well… no… it's not exactly a game. It's something you use for playing another game: hide-and-seek! Players scatter and hide with clattering cans on their feet – you'll see what happens!

It couldn't be simpler. Everyone takes 4 cans (from now on we're going to refer to them by their official name: "clatterers"). Gather up lots of pebbles, and put 10 of these in each clatterer. Tape the openings of the clatterers closed with the tape. Attach 2 clatterers to each of your feet, just like in this drawing (you can attach them with masking tape or duct tape. Don't spare the tape – make sure they won't fall off.) Are you ready? Let's play hide-and-seek! Oh! What an awful racket! The seeker can hear exactly where you've run to while he's counting to fifty with his eyes closed. Walking isn't easy either. Scatter with your clatterers carefully! Don't fall on your faces!

Hodge Podge

Hodge Podge is played in the classroom and all the kids in the class have to take part. But watch out! Make sure the teacher doesn't catch you! You'll never hear the end of it!

In *Hodge Podge*, the kids in your class participate by passing along stuff they've taken from their backpacks. For example, the starting person passes (oops, podges) an eraser to his neighbor. That classmate adds something from her backpack, and then podges both onto the next person. Everyone continues to add something from his or her backpack. More and more stuff gets podged along. All this stuff comprises the *Hodge Podge Pile*. The person who can't hold the pile of stuff in their hands anymore and drops something is out.

Be careful! The person who's handing over the pile is also out! Two people always lose together, so when you're podging the pile to one of your classmates, warn them "handle with care!" so they don't mess up!

If you can't pass the pile farther because nobody is sitting next to you then (sorry) that really big pile of stuff goes back the same direction it came. How long can the game go on before somebody is out? Figure out the best (sneakiest) way to play *Hodge Podge* in your classroom, without the teacher finding out! Happy *hodge podging*... troublemakers!

Jeu de Shoes

What will you need?

* the shoes you're wearing
* other people who are also wearing shoes
* at least one person with shoelaces in their shoes

Do you suffer from footsie-tosis? Then *Jeu de Shoes* isn't for you. In order to play this game you have to remove your shoes and it's strictly forbidden to beat your opponent with smelly feet. We're very sorry, but kids with stinky feet are just out of luck!

Everyone takes off their shoes. One of the players also has to take the shoelaces out of her shoes. One of her shoelaces is placed on the ground in a straight line. All the players have to stand behind this line. The ends of the other shoelace are tied together. This is now tossed to land where it likes, just like in that old fashioned French game, *Jeu de Boules* (the name sounds really elegant but it's just lawn bowling). In our version you don't bowl, you toss the shoelace onto the lawn. You also don't try to hit the shoelace with small silver balls, but with your shoes.

Everyone gets to throw twice: once with your left shoe and once with your right shoe. The person who gets his shoe closest to the shoelace circle wins the round. Like in *Jeu de Boules*, you're thinking? No, no, this is different. You'll see! For one thing, with shoes it can be dangerous if some nincompoop doesn't use the pooper scooper and then your shoe accidentally goes plop in the poop. But the real difference? You don't use your hands in *Jeu de Shoes*. Why would you? It's not called *Jeu de Gloves*. You have to throw your shoes with your feet! Good luck!

Sugar Shuffle

Sorry. We're sooooo terribly sorry. We've known about this game for years. It's such a treat, and we're only just getting around to telling you about it now. It's *Sugar Shuffle*, though some people call it *Sugar Puff*, because it takes a whole lot of puffing to play this game.

You'll need this:

* a little pile of sugar
* 2 drinking straws
* a tray
* a sheet of paper
* a marker
* Scotch® brand tape (or similar)
* and yes, someone to play with

Using a felt tip pen or a marker, divide a piece of paper into small squares, just like on a chessboard. Choose 4 of the boxes and color them black. It's completely up to you which boxes you choose. Next, tape the sheet of paper to a serving tray. Now take the sugar and sprinkle a layer of it across the piece of paper. The layer should be exactly the same thickness across the entire sheet. The game can begin!

In a little while there shouldn't be a single grain of sugar left on any of the black squares. In order to do this both of you take turns puffing through the straw. With each turn you're only allowed to puff once. If all 4 black squares are completely clean after your turn, then you've won (the other person is out). Is this game too easy? Make more black squares! One more rule: puff through your straw, okay? No drooling! Otherwise you'll have a slobbery mess instead of a game.

Noisy Nonsense

What will you need?

* moans and groans like "aaah!" and "oooh!"
* someone else to moan along

Noisy Nonsense is absolutely the weirdest and noisiest game you'll ever play. "S oooh! w aah! tch oooh ut!"

Here we go. Make up a sentence. For example, you could say "I can not think of a good sentence." It doesn't matter; all the players just have to remember the exact wording of your sentence for later on. Next, take turns letting out a good groan! You, for example, moan **"aaah!"** as loudly and as weirdly as you can. After that, you simply repeat the sentence you made up. But wait! Your groaning sound began with the letter **"a"**. This means that all the **"a"s** in the sentence have to be replaced with that same groan. So then it becomes, **"I c aaah! not think of aaah! good sentence!"** There are 2 **"a"s** in this sentence so you have to use the groan twice. And don't forget – the groans in your sentence have to be just as loud and just as weird as when you first moaned them!

Now it's someone else's turn. That player adds another groan to the same sentence – something like **"oooh!"** This groan begins with an **"o"**. He or she has to repeat the sentence with **aaah!** in place of **"a"** (just like you did or even weirder) and with **"oooh!"** in place of **"o"**. Other groans continue to be added to the sentence in the same way. Of course, the sentence gets weirder and weirder. It might eventually sound like: **"I c aaah! nooo! nooo! t thi nooo! k oooh! f aaah! g oooh! oooh! d s eeeh! nooo! t eeeh! nooo! c eeeh!"** You'll laugh your heads off playing this game. But be careful! If you forget even one letter or groan you're immediately out. So pay close attention while you're moaning and groaning like a weirdo, okay?

Enough Stuff

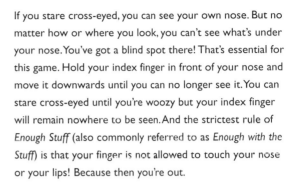

What will you need?

* nothing
* nobody (what a relief)

You're all alone on a deserted island. All your stuff is gone. You think back to all the outrageous games you read about in this book. Now what? Play something! (It's better than crying!) How about *Enough Stuff*? A game particularly suited to emergencies like this.

If you stare cross-eyed, you can see your own nose. But no matter how or where you look, you can't see what's under your nose. You've got a blind spot there! That's essential for this game. Hold your index finger in front of your nose and move it downwards until you can no longer see it. You can stare cross-eyed until you're woozy but your index finger will remain nowhere to be seen. And the strictest rule of *Enough Stuff* (also commonly referred to as *Enough with the Stuff*) is that your finger is not allowed to touch your nose or your lips! Because then you're out.

Now you need to go and do something. So, while you're wandering around in circles trying to come up with a rescue plan, keep gazing cross-eyed at your nose. If your finger hits your nose or your lips you're out! Oh no... you accidentally caught a glimpse of your finger? You're out too!

There's nobody around to keep an eye on you, which makes it easy to cheat! It's your call! If you're not completely honest, well... the only person you're cheating is you. So be tough on yourself! How long can you keep playing? This game is a cinch for people with big noses. Oh, you've got one of those cute little button noses? Oh well...

Ordinary Objects Index

Have you got lots of stuff? Use this index to see what you can do with it!

Stuff that will come in handy:

- air conditioning, 35
- backpack (filled with stuff), 37
- bags of potato chips, 14
- books, 14, 24
- bottle caps (different colors), 30
- brooms, 32
- buckets, 16
- calendars, 21
- cardboard, 15, 31
- cassette tape boxes, 29
- cassette tape player, 7
- CD player, 7
- chalk, 32
- cheese, 23
- chessboard, 22
- clock, 28
- dice, 21, 26, 34
- duct tape, 17, 36
- erasers, 34
- fence or ledge, 30
- film canisters
  (the plastic kind, with lids), 9
- floor lamp, 29
- fruit bowl, 25
- game pieces, 21, 34
- ice cubes (at least 20), 35
- index fingers
  (yours and other people's), 15
- junk mail flyers, 19
- kitchen scale, 12

- loose-leaf binders, 32
- marbles, 13, 25
- markers, 19, 21, 24, 26, 34, 39
- masking tape, 25, 36
- messy room, 9
- mop, 32
- pan lids, 18
- paper, 12, 14, 19, 24, 25, 28, 39
- pebbles (or stones), 36
- pencils, 24, 34
- pens, 12, 14, 25
- photo tabs, 12
- ping-pong ball, 22
- plastic cups, 16
- plastic soda bottles
  (empty 2 liter ones), 13
- plates, 23, 28, 32
- postal scale, 12
- push pins, 22
- rake, 32
- remote control, 20
- room (full of furniture), 7, 10
- rope, 17
- rubber bands, 11, 22
- ruler, 34
- salt, 39
- scissors, 15, 28
- Scotch® brand tape or similar, 24, 29, 39
- shoe laces, 38
- shoes, 38
- small ball, 15

- small stuff
  (doesn't matter what, as long
  as it's small), 12, 31
- socks (loose-fitting), 16
- soda cans (empty), 36
- spray bottle, 30
- state road map, 34
- sticky labels, 25, 31
- stopwatch, 16, 28
- straws (bendable), 23, 28, 39
- string, 11, 18, 29, 34
- stuff (doesn't matter what), 6
- sugar, 39
- T-shirts, 6
- table, 15, 24
- tennis balls, 17, 24, 32
- things with long handles, 32
- timer, 8, 16, 28
- toilet paper, 7, 26
- (empty) toilet paper tubes, 11
- toothpicks, 25
- toy people
  (Lego®, Playmobil®, etc.), 18, 22
- tray, 39
- umbrellas with curved handles, 32
- watch, 9, 16, 28
- water, 16
- wok, 25
- wooden blocks, 11
- wooden spoon (large), 24

Stuff that tends to break easily:

- antique pottery, 32
- crystal glasses, 32
- good china, 32
- priceless vases, 29, 32
- televisions, 20

Kinds of people you might need:

- an entire class, 37
- good guessers, 6, 8
- helpful grownup, 13
- klutzes (or clods), 15
- other people who want to play,
  7, 8, 11, 15, 16, 17, 25, 26, 28, 32, 34, 36, 38
- people wearing shoes, 38
- people who aren't sore losers, 34
- people who don't lose their cool, 35
- people who like playing hide-and-seek, 36
- people who like playing tag, 11
- people who like to bet, 25
- people who like to moan and groan, 40
- people who like to play soccer, 17
- people you can beat, 16
- referees, 10

- sharpshooters, 30
- someone else who wants to play,
  6, 7, 8, 9, 10, 12, 14, 18, 19, 20, 21, 22, 23, 24, 25, 26, 28, 29, 30, 31, 32, 34, 35, 38, 39, 40
- someone with shoelaces in their shoes, 38
- someone with ten fingers (not 9), 20
- someone who isn't a sore loser, 34
- teachers who don't notice very much, 37
- (worthy) opponents, 9, 13, 22, 24, 29
- yourself (so you can practice),
  7, 8, 9, 11, 13, 14, 16, 18, 19, 20, 22, 23, 24, 25, 28, 29, 30, 31, 32, 35, 36, 38, 39, 40, 41